LiHl

ℛℛ
RAVETTE PUBLISHING

ISBN: 978-1-84161-301-7

This edition first published in 2008 by
Ravette Publishing Limited
Unit 3, Tristar Centre, Star Road,
Partridge Green, West Sussex RH13 8RA
United Kingdom

Written by Gordon Volke

INTRODUCTION

Say, When Do They Begin?

So said Groucho Marx, watching a cricket match at Lord's.

If you don't agree with him and find cricket exciting, this book's not for you.

If you passionately hate cricket and will always hate cricket as long as the Pope remains Catholic, this book's not for you either.

But if you wish you liked cricket so you could share your partner's passion for the game, then this book's just what you want!

The WAGs Little Book of Cricket is aimed at the Wives and Girlfriends of male cricket-lovers of every kind. He may be the type who spends the whole of a Saturday watching a County Cricket match when he could go shopping with you. He could also be a player for the local team who spends all of Sunday afternoon on the pitch and the rest of the evening in the pub instead of taking the kids out and giving you a break. Or, worst of all, he could be a keen Test match buff who lies on the sofa for five days at a stretch watching every ball and who gets up in the middle of the night to follow every detail of the tour Down-Under.

Whatever category of cricket-fanatic your partner belongs to, the common denominator is that you're not part of the equation. So the answer's simple – gen up a bit on cricket and start to join in. He'll look at you with new eyes if he doesn't have to explain some simple rule to you at the moment the batsman is scoring his century or the wicket-keeper is making a spectacular diving catch.

So please read and repeat out loud—

Cricket is not boring. I will get to like the game.

And so you shall if you work your way through the sections that follow. In a witty and waggish way, you'll learn all you need to know about cricket so that you can start to enjoy the game. Helping the medicine go down even further are lots of jokes and quotes and funny cricketing anecdotes, plus a handy inventory of cricketing terms arranged in alphabetical order.

This is an invitation that should bowl a maiden over.

Come on, then. Roll out the googlies!

HISTORY OF CRICKET

What a Load of Old (Bat and) Balls

Bit of a problem here. We're agreed you find cricket a tad boring, so you're going to find the history of cricket mind-blowingly, lose-the-will-to-live, screamingly boring! At the same time, you need to know the origins of the game if you're going to become a knowledgeable Cricket-WAG.

What's the answer? Info-bytes! They're the intellectual equivalent of chicken nuggets, but even more digestible and better for your health …

a) Nobody quite knows where the game of cricket began. Some people think it developed from ancient bat-and-ball games brought from India by merchants. Others believe it began as a game played by children in Kent and Sussex during Saxon or Norman times.

b) The name 'cricket' is equally confusing. It could be a variant of the French word *criquet* which means 'a club' and is linked to the game of croquet. Alternatively, it could come from the Dutch word *krick* which means 'a stick' or the old English word cricc which means 'a staff of wood'.

c) The first recorded reference to the game occurs in 1597 during a court case in Guildford, Surrey. A dispute over land belonging to the Royal Grammar School cites the sport of *kreckett* being played there.

d) Village cricket played by adults seems to have begun around the 1650s. Up until then, the game was still played mainly by children.

e) The laws of cricket were laid down in 1744 and amended in 1774. During this period, the game became very popular with aristocratic gentlemen who gambled heavily on the outcome of matches.

f) Cricket travelled to India, South Africa, Australia and New Zealand by way of the British Empire. This was a terrible mistake because, ever since, the colonies have taken great delight at beating the Mother Country at her own game.

g) County cricket began during the first half of the 19th Century. The first County Championship matches were played in 1890.

h) The first International Match was played in 1844 between Canada and the USA in New Jersey.

i) The first Test matches took place between England and Australia in 1877 in Australia.

j) Shortly after, the Australians visited England for the first proper Overseas Cricket Tour. Then, in 1882, there was that famous match at the Oval in which the wicket was burned. England and Australia have been competing for The Ashes (the remains of the stumps in a diddy little urn) ever since.

There! That wasn't too bad, was it? I said, WASN'T TOO BAD, WAS IT? Oh! Sorry to wake you! So it *was* that bad! Never mind. It's over now and there's some fun stuff coming up next. So press on, eh?

CRICKET JOKES

Hit For Six!

Here are some cricketing jokes to put in your Cricket-WAGs repertoire and bring out next time you're at the bar ...

A spider walked out to bat.
"Not him again!" groaned the grasshopper.
"Isn't he any good?" asked the ant.
"Quite the opposite," replied the grasshopper. "He stays in for ever. The only way to get him out is leg-leg-leg-leg-leg-leg-leg-leg-before wicket!"

A cricket enthusiast had three trays installed in his office labelled 'In', 'Out' and 'LBW'.

A visitor remarked that he could see the significance of 'In' and 'Out', but what did 'LBW' mean?

And the cricket enthusiast replied …

"Let the Bastards Wait".

An expectant father rang the hospital to
see how his wife was getting on, but in
his excitement he dialled the number for
Lord's by mistake.

"How's it going?" he asked, eagerly.

"Fine," came the reply. "We've got two
out already and the rest should be out
before tea. The last one was a duck."

"You're looking glum."

"Yes. My doctor says I can't play
cricket."

"Really? I didn't know he'd ever seen
you play!"

An American was taken to watch a cricket match while he was visiting England. He watched with interest as the teams came out and the batsman scored a few runs off the first six balls. Then the umpire shouted, "OVER!"

"Gee," said the American getting up to leave. "It's a cool game – but it's mighty short!"

COMIC DEFINITION OF CRICKET

HOWZAT!

Right! Time to get down to the real nitty-gritty. Here's a clear and concise definition of cricket which you need to understand and remember …

You have two sides … one out in the field and one in.

Each player that's in the side that's in, goes out when he's out.

He comes in and the next player goes in until he's out.

When they are all out, the side that's out comes in and the side that's been in, goes out and tries to get those coming in, out.

Sometimes, you get players still in and not out.

When both sides have been in and out, including those not out, the game is over!

Okay? Got it? That's all you need to know about cricket … er, sorry?

You mean you *don't get it*?

Course you don't! Just our little joke! The real explanation of the game follows in the next section. Please read on!

BASICS OF THE GAME

Baseball On Valium

That was how the actor, Robin Williams, summed up cricket. But what does he know? If, like you, he'd read the following A to Z of cricket, he'd also start to love the sound of leather on willow …

a) A cricket pitch is approx 525 feet (160 metres) by 550 feet (170 metres).

b) The *wicket* consists of three wooden *stumps*, each 28 inches high with two short wooden *bails* balanced across the top. Two wickets are placed 66 feet (20.12 metres) apart, near the middle of the field.

c) The line in front of the wicket is called the *crease*. The batsmen risk being out if they do not remain behind this while the ball is in play.

d) The area surrounding the wickets is called the *outfield*.

e) The edge of the pitch is called the *boundary*. It is marked by a white line and/or little white blocks of wood.

f) The game is played between two teams of 11 players. One team bats while the other bowls.

g) Only two batsmen take to the crease at any one time, while the whole of the bowling team is on the field, trying to get the batsmen out.

h) The batsman is out if the bowler delivering the ball knocks down the bails of the batsman's wicket. This is called being *bowled*.

i) He is also out if the ball knocks his wicket over when he is out of his crease. This is called being *stumped*.

j) To be *caught*, the fielders must catch the ball hit by the batsman before it touches the ground.

k) Other ways of getting out are *run out, leg-before-wicket, hitting your own wicket, handling the ball, obstruction of the fielding side, hitting the ball twice* and *being timed out*.

l) The idea of the game is to score *runs*. One batsman hits the ball and then the two of them run between the wickets. Each time they pass each other, it scores one run.

m) Runs can also be scored without actually doing any running by hitting the ball over the boundary. If it rolls along the ground and crosses the boundary line, that scores *a four* (4 runs). A big hit that sends the ball out of play over the boundary line without touching the ground scores *a six* (6 runs).

n) Runs can also be added to the batting score without the batsman actually hitting it. These are called *extras*. There are four different kinds:- *byes* and *leg-byes* (when the ball goes past the batsman and is not stopped by the fielders), *wides* (when the ball is bowled out of the batsman's reach) and *no-balls* (when the bowler fails to bowl properly).

o) The eleven players coming in to bat one after the other is called an *innings*. Most cricket matches have one innings per side. Test matches have two.

p) The team which has scored more runs at the end of all the innings,

wins the match. Usually, the number of batsmen out is quoted with the score. So you will hear scores like ...
England 156 all out (156 runs for the loss of all eleven wickets) ...
Australia 604 for 3 (604 runs for the loss of only 3 wickets).

q) The bowler throws the ball overarm, which usually reaches the batsman on one bounce. After six bowls, the umpire calls "over" and another bowler bowls to the batsman at the other wicket.

r) A *fast bowler* charges up to the wicket and hurls the ball at the batsman in the most ferocious and terrifying manner possible.

s) A *spin bowler* sidles up to the wicket and bowls the ball slowly with a cunning spin on it, making it change direction when it hits the ground, which bamboozles the batsman.

t) The game is supervised by two *umpires* who make all the decisions as to whether a batsman is out or not. Their word is final and it is considered very bad form to show any dissent.

u) A cricket bat is made of *laminated willow* and the ball is covered with *stitched leather*.

v) Cricket teams have one substitute called *the twelfth man*. He is only allowed to field.

w) By their very nature, cricket matches are long affairs, so there is a *lunch interval* or a *tea interval* or both.

x) *Winning the toss* is vitally important in cricket. Matches can be won or lost by getting the choice of whether to bat first or bowl first.

y)   Often, neither side completely wins a game of cricket and it ends in a *draw*. This is not to be confused with a *tie* which is when both sides end up with exactly the same score (very rare!).

z)   Every cricket match, even the smallest village one, has an official *scorer*. This person keeps a proper tally of runs gained and wickets taken etc. The umpires use hand signals to tell the scorer when a four or a six has been scored or when the batsman is out.

Now, then. That was a bit more interesting, wasn't it?
Good. You've taken your first steps towards becoming a Cricket-WAG!

FUNNY COMMENTATING MISTAKES

Many A Slip

There are two kinds of cricketing *slips*. There's the fielding position and there are these funny mistakes made by commentators watching the game. Here are some of the latter ...

The bowler's Holding the batsman's Willey.

Brian Johnson

And Marshall throws his head into his hands.

Chris Martin-Jenkins

On the first day, Logie decided to chance his arm and it came off.

Trevor Bailey

He's got the guts to score runs when the crunch is down.

John Murray

Yorkshire 232 all out, Hutton ill ... I'm sorry, Hutton 111.

John Snagge

Anyone foolish enough to predict the outcome of this match is a fool.

Fred Trueman

In the back of Hughes' mind must be the thought that he will dance down the piss and mitch one.

Tony Greig

That slow motion replay doesn't show how fast the ball was travelling.

Richie Benaud

So that's 57 runs needed by Hampshire in 11 overs and it doesn't need a calculator to tell you that the run rate required is 5.1818.

Norman DeMesquita

The sight of Bright holds no fright for Wright.

Jim Maxwell

And Ian Greig's on eight, including two fours.

Jim Laker

For any budding cricketers listening, do you have any superstitious routines before an innings like putting one pad on first and then the other one?

Tony Lewis

The Queen's Park Oval, is exactly as the name suggests, absolutely round.

Tony Cozier

He'll certainly want to start by getting off the mark.

Don Mosey

That black cloud is coming from the direction the wind is blowing, now the wind is coming from where the black cloud is.

Ray Illingworth

FIELDING POSITIONS

Silly Mid-Wicket and Other Silly Stuff

When a team is fielding, the players stand in various positions on the field. Each position has its own name and these are used all the time when people talk about cricket. So you really need to know a bit about them if you're going to receive a proper Cricket-WAGs education …

Two Sides to Everything

Let's start with the basic terms, *off side* and *on side* (or *leg side*). The off side is that half of the field to the batsman's right. The on side (more usually called the leg side) is the other half of the field to his left. (For left-handers, reverse everything!)

Two to Tango

The fielding team must have a *bowler* getting the ball into play at one end and a *wicket keeper* stopping it going out of play at the other. Where the remaining nine players choose to stand, is entirely up to them.

Just a Slip of a Thing

The fielding position that's easiest to understand is the *slips*. This is a spot just behind the right of the batsman. Usually, two or three fielders stand here, waiting like vultures to catch any ball that nicks off the edge of the bat.

All Getting a Bit Deep

Any position round the edge of the pitch is known as *long* or *deep*. So if you hear these terms, you'll know they mean anywhere near the boundary, a long way from the batsman. *Long On, Long Off, Deep Fine Leg, Deep Extra Cover* are common examples.

What a Silly Billy

A fielding position very close to the batsman is called *silly*. (A more accurate term would be *f*****g dangerous*, but that's not gentlemanly enough for cricket.) Expect anyone fielding at *Silly Mid-On* or *Silly Point* to be carted off to hospital before the game is over.

Join the Inner Circle

The most-mentioned fielding positions occur in a circle about 30 yards around the pitch. So let's look at these in a bit more detail ...

Square Leg

This point is level with the batsman on his left-hand side. (One of the umpires also stands here because it gives the best view of the batsman and the stumps.)

Point

Directly opposite *square leg* – level with the batsman on his right-hand side.

Mid-Wicket and Cover

These are the same as *square leg* and *point*, but they are either side of the second batsman down at the other end of the pitch.

Gully
This is a position near the *slips* on the right-hand side. It prevents the ball being steered past the *slips* to the boundary.

Mid On and Mid Off
Two positions just behind where the bowler starts his run up. They stop the batsman hitting the ball straight back down the pitch.

There are other positions you'll probably hear mentioned like *Fine Leg* and *Third Man*, but don't worry too much about them. The others are the important ones.

Warning!
If you feel you'd like to know a lot more about fielding positions, beware! You're fast becoming a cricket anorak instead of a WAG. You need to take emergency action immediately ... go shopping!

FUNNY QUOTES ABOUT CRICKET

A Bit of Wit and Wisden

You're due for a spot of relaxation and recuperation after all that fielding business, so here are some funny and insightful quotes about the true nature of cricket.

(By the way, *Wisden* is the name of a Cricket Almanac that has been published annually since the year dot. It has nothing whatsoever to do with this next section other than to give it a pithy title.)

There is a widely held and quite
erroneous belief that cricket is just
another game.

Prince Philip

Cricket is the only game when you can
actually put on weight when playing.

Tommy Docherty

Cricket is like sex films. It relieves
frustration and tension.

Linda Lovelace

I don't like defensive shots. You can only
get threes.

W G Grace

It's a funny kind of month, October. For the really keen cricket fan, it's when you realise that your wife left you in May.

Dennis Norden

I am to cricket what Dame Sybil Thorndike is to non-ferrous welding.

Frank Muir

Cricket needs brightening up a bit. My solution is to let the players drink at the beginning of the game, not after. It always works in our picnic matches.

Paul Hogan

Neil Harvey's at slip, with his legs wide apart, waiting for a tickle.

Brian Johnson

To have some idea what it's like *(to be a batsman facing a fast bowler)*, stand in the outside lane of a motorway, get your mate to drive his car at you at 95 miles an hour and wait until he's 12 yards away before you decide which way to jump.

Geoff Boycott

GLOSSARY OF CRICKETING TERMS

England Will Win if Camilla Parker Bowls

So said an Australian fan's banner some years ago. Australian cricket-watchers are among the keenest in the world. They understand the game and know all the jargon that goes with it. *But do you?*

Of course you don't! You're still a beginner. But here's your chance to change all that – a waggish glossary of all the major cricketing terms arranged in alphabetical order for quick ready-reference.

Enjoy!

Asking Rate
This means number of runs per over that the team batting second needs to score in order to beat the total set by the team that batted first.

Ball Tampering
A form of cheating (very frowned upon) in which the bowler slightly damages the ball to make it behave unpredictably.

Beamer
Even more frowned upon … a
dangerous ball from a fast bowler that
flies straight towards the batsman's head
in the hope of knocking it off his
shoulders. (Also called *Chin Music.*)

Bouncer (or Bumper)
Another act of aggressive bowling. This
time, the ball is pitched very short so
that it rears up and hits the batsman or
makes him duck.

Bunny (or a Rabbit)
A player who's a brilliant bowler or wicket-keeper, but can't bat to save his life. Usually goes in last.

Bunsen
Term used to describe a wicket that favours spin bowlers. (Comes from the Cockney rhyming slang of Bunsen Burner - meaning a 'turner'.)

Carrying Your Bat
An opening batsman who's still in at the end of the innings when all his other team mates are out.

Century

One batsman scoring 100 runs (or more) in a single innings.

Corridor of Uncertainty

No, this doesn't describe a young cricketer making his first visit to a brothel. It means the area, just to the right of the batsman, where he can't be sure whether to hit the ball or leave it to go past harmlessly.

Cow Corner

A lovely phrase meaning a fielding position right on the edge of the boundary, miles away from play.

Dibbly-Dobbly Bowlers

An even better name meaning medium-pace bowlers who bowl in such a way that the batsmen find it hard to score many runs.

Declaring/Making The Declaration

Nothing to do with undying love! Sometimes, the batting team makes so many runs that they want to stop their innings before all of their batsmen are out. So they *declare*. (It's a phrase you'll hear all the time.)

Delivery
The proper term for bowling the ball.

Dolly or Dolly Drop
A very easy catch.

Duck
A batsman scores a *duck* if he is out without scoring any runs. (Also sometimes called a *Blob*.) If the match has two innings per side and the batsman scores 0 on both occasions, this is known as *Bagging a Pair*. And if you're out first ball in both innings, that's a *King Pair!*

Duckworth Lewis Method

Sounds like a form of contraception, but actually it's a cunning mathematical system that decides the winner of one-day cricket matches that have been interrupted by rain.

Full Toss

A ball from the bowler that does not bounce before it reaches the batsman. Usually gets whacked for six.

Gardening

You often see batsmen doing this – wandering down the wicket between balls and prodding the ground with the end of their bat. They are flattening bumps and repairing holes that might make the ball bounce awkwardly.

Googly

A sneaky type of spin bowling that makes the ball change direction and fool the batsman.

Hat Trick

Everyone knows that a hat-trick is when someone scores three in a row. But did you know that the phrase originates from cricket? Years ago, when a bowler took three wickets with successive balls, he was given a hat in recognition of his outstanding skill.

Hawk-Eye

Not a nickname for the umpire or a Native American cricketer, this is a piece of modern technology designed to clarify difficult leg-before-wicket decisions.

Howzat? (How's that? or How is he?)
This is what the bowler and the fielders
ask the umpire if they think the batsman
is out. It's also known as *appealing* –
although there's nothing very appealing
about the way they shout and yell the
question! The reason they have to keep
demanding to know, is that the umpire is
not obliged to say that the batsman is out
unless he is asked.

Jaffa
A brilliant delivery from the bowler that
completely fools the batsman and
usually gets him out.

Knocking Up
Warming up before a match. (What did you think it meant?)

Length
Cricket commentators bang on all the time about this. It means where the ball bounces down the wicket. So you'll hear phrases like *short length, good length* or *full length.*

Lollipop
A ball that is really easy to hit.

Maiden Over

This is the name given to an over in which the bowler delivers all six balls without the batsman scoring a run. (So when you hear a bowler's figures after an innings, it will be something like ... 20 overs, 4 maidens, 6 for 154, which means ... 'bowled a total of 20 overs - in 4 of them, the batsman didn't score any runs ... the bowler took 6 wickets at the expense of 154 runs'.)

Middle (or To Middle It)

A powerful stroke that hits the ball right in the middle of the bat and sends it a very long way.

Nelson and Double Nelson

This is a bit rude. Legend has it that Lord Nelson's 'third leg' was said to be almost as long as his other two, making him look like a cricket wicket! A score of 111 also resembles three stumps, so it is named after him - and 222 is twice that. For some inexplicable reason, both scores are thought to be unlucky.

Nervous Nineties

Batsmen feel under pressure when they get close to scoring a century.

New Ball
The ball is changed after 80 overs. It is usually an advantage to the bowler because the new ball is shinier and more bouncy.

Nightwatchman
Batsmen who are still in at the end of a day's play *or* a weaker batsman put in to bat in the closing overs instead of a good batsman who can be saved for the following day.

No-Balls
According to the famous song, Goebbels had this problem. So do bowlers who

step over the front crease when delivering the ball. It gives a run to the batting side.

Occupying the Crease
This simply means a batsman who avoids taking any chances and does not get himself out, usually to play out time and end the match in a draw.

Playing On
Not to be confused with playing away, this is when a batsman mis-hits the ball and it diverts onto his stumps, getting himself out.

Reverse Sweep
A very unorthodox shot in which the batsman drops to one knee and hits the ball in the opposite direction from the one you would expect. Can look sensational and score a lot of runs. Can also easily get you out!

Rippers
Cricketers are too gentlemanly to fart loudly in the changing rooms, so this term means deliveries by a fast bowler who also puts a strong spin on the ball.

Rock
Nickname for the ball.

Rough

No, not 'a bit of rough'. Cricketers are also too gentlemanly to be a bit of rough. This term applies to the little patch of ground that gets scuffed up at either end as the bowlers finish their run. This patch of uneven ground can be exploited by the spin bowlers as the game progresses.

Runner

If a batsman is hurt but can continue batting, he can use another player to do his running for him. The runner must wear pads just like the batsman.

Seam

The *seam* is the thick row of stitching around the ball. When the ball hits the ground on the seam, it tends to change direction. Bowlers who use this to their advantage are called *seam bowlers* or *seamers*.

Shouldering Arms

You often see batsmen do this. They decide the ball coming towards them does not want to be hit, so they lift their bat high in the air with both arms to get it out of the way.

Sitter

Similar to a *dolly*, this is an easy catch that should never be dropped. To do so is called *missing a sitter* and is very embarrassing indeed.

Sledging

A strange term bearing no relation to ice and snow. It means talking to the batsman between delivering, insulting him and making him annoyed in the hope that he will lose concentration and give his wicket away cheaply. Some of the banter can be very funny. On other occasions it can be very aggressive and offensive.

Swing Bowling
This type of delivery curves through the air as it approaches the batsman. This is quite different from seam bowling which relies on the ball hitting the ground to fool the batsman.

Tailenders
Players who go in to bat towards the end of an innings. Usually, they are the bowlers and the wicket keeper. So they are not as good at batting as the regular batsmen who go in at the beginning.

Throwing
Allowed when fielding but not when bowling. The arm must be kept quite

straight to make a proper delivery. (Not to be confused with *throwing up* which is what you do round the back of the pavilion after about 15 pints.)

Ton
Slang for scoring a century.

Two-Paced
No, it doesn't say *two-faced* – cricketers aren't cads and bounders who'd say one thing and mean another. They're decent chaps, through-and-through! This phrase refers to a Test match wicket that has been played on for four or five days. The ground is beginning to break up, so

sometimes the ball bounces slowly and on other occasions it shoots towards the batsman like a rocket.

Walking

This proves our point. Sometimes, batsmen are not given out by the umpire when they know themselves that they nicked the ball with the bat and have been caught in the slips. So they *walk* or give themselves out – a noble, honest and self-sacrificing gesture akin to The Charge of The Light Brigade.

Wide

You know already that this is an extra (a run being added to the batting score as a result of the bowler delivering the ball so far away from the batsman that he cannot play it). It also results in the ball being bowled again, so overs with *wides* in them can contain seven, eight or even more balls.

Yorker

The delivery every batsman dreads! The ball is bowled full-toss at his toes and usually ends up knocking over his stumps.

ENGLISH CRICKET GROUNDS

Grounds For Divorce

Keen cricketing types show more love and devotion to their cricket grounds than they do to their wives. More than any other sport, they worship their bits of hallowed turf with great reverence and regard all the well-known cricket venues as their spiritual homes.

From your point of view, this is a pain because it means you also need to be clued-up on these places. So here's a brief run-down of the six major English cricket grounds …

Lord's

Named after Thomas Lord, who founded the original site in the 1780s, this is the 'home' of English cricket. Now situated in St John's Wood Road near Regent's Park in London, it's the HQ of a number of important cricketing organisations:-

- The International Cricket Conference (world governing body)

- The Cricket Council and The Test and County Cricket Board (controllers of English cricket)

- The Marylebone Cricket Club (or MCC, another ruling body)

- Middlesex County Cricket Club

As you can imagine, there's quite an old-boy network here. As Fred Trueman, the famous fast bowler, once remarked when asked if he'd seen the dinosaurs in *Jurassic Park* ? "I could go to any committee room if I wanted to see that."

The (Brit) Oval
In south London, near Vauxhall Bridge. Home of Surrey County Cricket Club.

Trent Bridge
Nottinghamshire County Cricket Club play here. It has a huge pavilion that was used as a military hospital during the First World War and the main Army postal sorting office during the Second.

Old Trafford
Near to Manchester United's football ground of the same name. Officially, the wettest cricket venue in the country. English bowler, Jim Laker, took all 10 wickets in a Test match here in 1956. Lancashire CCC's ground.

Edgbaston
In Birmingham. Warwickshire CCC play here.

Headingly
Home of Yorkshire CCC.

COMPETITIONS AND TEAMS

Two Men and a Dog

Traditionally, these were the spectators at a County Cricket match. This has all changed recently - a cat after the pigeons on the pitch joined them last year.

Actually, professional cricket at all levels draws large crowds, so you need to know about the various competitions in case you find yourself in one of them ...

County Set

The County Championships take place every year. The County Cricket Clubs all play each other and the matches, which last for more than one day, take place on a regular basis throughout the summer. Teams amass points, just like in the Football League.

It's a Knockout

Also like the FA Cup, there is a knockout cup competition which is usually named after its sponsor such as *Gillette* or *NatWest*. These are all one-day games. The final is a colourful occasion played in a packed ground in front of two enthusiastic sets of supporters.

20/20 Vision

A recent development to try to draw in bigger crowds is called *20/20 cricket*. Here, teams are restricted to only 20 overs, so they have to take chances and score lots of runs right from the start. The idea is to make the match short and very exciting to watch.

Very Testing

Test matches are international games that last for five days. Each team has two innings. They are played when overseas teams visit England and vice versa. The big names in Test cricket are:-
Australia, New Zealand, India, Pakistan, Sri Lanka, England, South Africa and The West Indies.

The World's Your Oyster
The Cricket World Cup is an international tournament of one-day cricket played every 4 years.

Interesting Note -
County cricket and Test cricket is played with a *red* ball ... one-day cricket is played with a *white* one.

FAMOUS NAMES

He Puts It Where He Likes

This is what well-known Victorian bowler, J C Shaw, said about the greatest cricketer of all time, W G Grace. The phrase is true of all the great cricketers, batsmen or bowlers. So here are a few famous names to store away in your Cricket-WAGs memory and bring out at a suitable time …

William Gilbert Grace

Most people are familiar with the portly and heavily bearded figure of the 'father of English cricket'. Despite being a doctor, he played first-class cricket for 43 years, scoring nearly 55,000 runs and 126 centuries. He was also a formidable bowler with a tally of 2,876 wickets. He played in the first ever Test match against Australia in September 1880 and was the first Englishman to score a Test century in that game.

Len Hutton
Legendary batsman of the inter-war years. In 1938, he scored 364 as England beat Australia by the highest Test score ever - 903 for 7 declared.

Don Bradman
The great Australian batsman of the
same period.

Fred Trueman
A terrifying English fast bowler of the
Fifties and Sixties. A colourful
Yorkshireman who was never afraid to
speak his mind. He later became an
amusing cricket commentator. The
working title of his autobiography was
*The Definitive Volume On The Finest Bloody
Fast Bowler That Ever Drew Breath.*

Sir Garfield Sobers
The first batsman to score the maximum
possible from a single over – 36 runs (six
sixes in a row) in 1968.

Geoff Boycott
Another outspoken Yorkshireman, this time famous for his stubborn batting. As someone once said of him … "Geoff Boycott's idea of bliss might be to bat all night, having batted all day." He is now a well-known cricket commentator, admired for his cricketing insight, no-nonsense attitudes and scathing wit.

David Gower
The white-haired team captain in the early series of *They Think It's All Over*. A natural and elegant stroke-player. Scored 8,231 runs in 117 Test appearances.

Ian Botham

The chap from the *Shredded Wheat* ads who bangs on about having a healthy heart. He was an awesome all-rounder who could win matches almost on his own. As a bowler, he took 383 Test wickets between 1977 and 1992, one of the highest totals of all time.

Brian Lara

This West Indian batsman holds two amazing records - the highest individual Test score ever (375 runs) and the highest individual County level score ever (501 not out).

Andrew (Freddie) Flintoff
The current England fast bowler and superstar.

Shane Warne
Recently retired Australian bowling sensation. A larger-than-life character whose colourful lifestyle often hit the headlines, he became the first bowler ever to take 700 Test wickets.

QUIZ

End of the Innings

Your day of reckoning has come! All the witty and waspish info has been imparted and it's time to see how much you have remembered.

Here are 15 light-hearted questions to test your 'cricket-ology'. Score *one run* for every question answered correctly. Then check your Cricket-WAG qualification level against our special scoreboard.

1. What is an *Extra?*

   a) a run added to the batting team's score
   b) an actor in a film about cricket
   c) gum chewed by cricketers

2. What's the name of the famous Victorian cricketer with the bushy beard?

   a) Larry Grayson
   b) Gracie Fields
   c) W G Grace

3. Fill in the missing letters to complete this sentence ...

The little wooden rods that balance on the top of the stumps are called the b - - - s.

4. Rearrange the letters to spell the word that means to insult a batsman in the hope of making him lose his concentration ...

D N G L S I E G

5. Yorkshire County Cricket Club home ground is Old Trafford

a) True
b) False

6. What is a *beamer?*

a) a cricketer who smiles a lot
b) an aggressive and dangerous type of bowling
c) an expensive German car

7. When was the first written reference made to *krekett* being played by schoolboys in Guildford, Surrey?

   a) 1357
   b) 1597
   c) 1777

8. What word or phrase does the fielding side shout at the umpire to see if the batsman is out?

9. In 1968, who hit six sixes in a row to score a maximum 36 runs off one over?

   a) Sir Garfield Sobers
   b) Ian Botham
   c) Andrew Flintoff

10. What is *The Twelfth Man*?

   a) a Shakespeare play
   b) an old black and white film starring Orson Welles
   c) a cricket team's only substitute

11. What are *the slips?*

    a) a fielding position just behind
       the batsman
    b) a wet and skiddy wicket
    c) what cricketers dress up in on a
       Saturday night

12. What is the name of the fielder who
    wears gloves and stands behind the
    stumps, catching the ball?

13. Where is Lord's cricket ground?

    a) Manchester
    b) London
    c) Bognor Regis

14. Complete the name of the Australian fast bowler who recently became the first player to take 700 Test wickets

    - - - - - Warne

15. What happens when a batting team
declares?

   a) the players express their love for
      one another
   b) the game is abandoned and
      everyone goes down the pub
   c) the team wants to end its innings
      before all the batsmen are out

Answers

1. a) a run added to the batting team's score
2. c) W G Grace
3. bails
4. SLEDGING
5. b) False (it's the home of Lancashire CCC)
6. b) an aggressive and dangerous type of bowling
7. b) 1597
8. HOWZAT or HOW IS HE?
9. a) Sir Garfield Sobers
10. c) a cricket team's only substitute
11. a) a fielding position just behind the batsman
12. the Wicket Keeper
13. b) London
14. Shane (Warne)
15. c) the team wants to end its innings before all the batsmen are out

Scoreboard

0 - 5 runs
Well done.
You have passed your Cricket-WAGs
course at Elementary level.

6 - 10 runs
Excellent.
You have passed your Cricket-WAGs
course at Intermediate level.

11 - 15 runs
Many congratulations!
You have passed your Cricket-WAGs
course at Advanced level.

Alternative Ending

Right! That's your lot. Either you've converted to cricket by now, or you're still bored. If it's the latter, here's an escape route for you ...

Don't be a Cricket-WAG, just be a WAG!

Here's how to qualify ...

* wear huge designer sunglasses
* keep your tan topped up
* know where the cameras are and have a pout ready for them at all times
* never be seen without full make-up, even when popping out for the paper

- ★ use your mobile phone as often as you can, especially for taking photos
- ★ shop 'til you drop and make sure you're seen carrying bags from the most expensive boutiques
- ★ drive a chunky 4-wheel-drive off-roader or sportscar
- ★ make sure you appear in *Hello* or *OK* magazines as often as possible
- ★ have the occasional falling-out with your fellow WAGs
- ★ only go to the trendiest nightclubs
- ★ pretend to like sport
- ★ *hate* all sport

And if you can't afford all this … just go back to being you!